SOCIAL
PEDAGOGY

AN INVITATION

POCKET BOOK

Author: Manuel Kaska, social pedagogue and
social worker, social pedagogy training facilitator
and consultant, Jacaranda

Author's critical friend: Robert Braun, social pedagogue
and social worker, social pedagogy training facilitator
and consultant, Jacaranda

Editor: Abby Ladbrooke, founder Jacaranda

Editor's critical friend: Doug Lawson, social worker
and independent consultant

First published in 2015 by:
Jacaranda Development,
a trading name of Jacaranda Recruitment Ltd
The Leathermarket, Weston Street, London SE1 3ER
Telephone: 020 3384 0989
info@jacaranda-development.co.uk
jacaranda-development.co.uk

A catalogue record for this book is available from the British Library.
ISBN: 978-0-9932714-0-3

Design & layout by designrabrooks.com
Printed by unitedprint.com UK Ltd. London

Further details about Jacaranda can be found at
jacaranda-development.co.uk and we are pleased
to hear from you in person, by phone, post or email.

CONTENTS

ACKNOWLEDGEMENTS

Thank you to all our colleagues who have offered their thoughts and advice on this project. Special thanks to Bianka Lang, Fran Pretsch and Nadine De Simone, social pedagogues who all have considerable experience in UK statutory services, whose insights and comments have been invaluable. Thanks to all other members of the Jacaranda team for everything we have learned from each other over the years, with particular thanks to Thure Johansen whose creativity and reflective prompts have been a special source of inspiration and development. Many thanks to Naeomi Randles for her endless patience in navigating the unfamiliar waters of publishing and Ingolf Block for his flow of ideas and unwavering support as a colleague and co-founder since 2003.

Thank you to colleagues in the Social Pedagogy Consortium for comments on specific areas of the book, and for our stimulating collaboration more generally.

We would also like to thank every participant of our learning and development courses; you have quite simply been our biggest source of inspiration.

INTRODUCTION

Developments in social pedagogy have gained pace in recent years. Increasing numbers of people attend the Social Pedagogy Development Network (p.33 Developments in the UK and Ireland), more organisations are commissioning work-based learning and development courses, and growing numbers of degree qualified social pedagogues are employed. More higher education institutions are introducing social pedagogy into their curricula. There is increasing evidence of improved outcomes and we hear more and more stories of the impact of social pedagogy beyond traditional outcome measures. We also hear that social pedagogy resonates with the original reasons people started work in the caring professions.

In the context of the development of social pedagogy in the UK and Ireland, we have understood that a concise introduction to social pedagogy in this format is, for a number of reasons, a preferred starting point for some. We hope this both responds to and expands the curiosity that led you to this resource. In social pedagogy there is much to know, feel and do, so there is scope to be "constantly curious", which is perhaps a defining characteristic of social pedagogy. We believe you may recognise some things, reframe and refresh and learn new.

We aim also to make you aware of the rich and diverse ways to find out more. Those developing social pedagogy, as well as growing in number, are open. In our experience people are happy to share their knowledge and experiences. Signposts to networking events, learning and development opportunities, books, research and academic papers, web-links and newsletters can be found at the end of this book.

It is safe to say, we have approached the creation of a "pocket book" with some level of caution. We see the need for it, and at the same time have asked ourselves if the very *existence* of it conveys a message we would not intend to communicate. (p.71 Communication; p.55 Reflection). It could be perceived as reducing something incredibly rich and multifaceted, and this is not our intention. In our view this book finds a healthy balance between being concise and being an invitation to further exploration. It aims to be approachable and to provide a flavour of social pedagogy, with an emphasis on introducing more people to the approach. If we succeed in providing a springboard for further exploration, we will have achieved our main aim.

HOW TO USE THIS BOOK

This pocket book is written for a wide audience: practitioners, carers, commissioners, care staff, managers, supervisors, policy makers, funders, and so on. It may make sense to read it from cover to cover; dipping into isolated parts would come with an invitation to keep dipping!

Understanding social pedagogy takes time and can be achieved in many ways; experientially, in observation, in dialogue, and via courses, for example, as well as by reading. A wide range of concepts, theories and ideas inform social pedagogy. They are underpinned and held together by values that emphasise potential, development, learning and positive regard for people.

Social pedagogy is a holistic approach in which particular methods or other specific approaches may be chosen with social pedagogical thought and according to the context. (Hämäläinen, 2003). It is both a way of thinking and viewing things *and* an amalgam of tools and concepts. It works with and for individuals, groups, communities and society at large. To read some parts without the others, and indeed to read only this pocket book, will give only a partial understanding of social pedagogy. Whilst tempting, and possibly beneficial if some elements are put into practice, most can be gained from a wider, more encompassing understanding.

As you read we hope you will recognise the values of social pedagogy within the concepts we have introduced, and you may also start to see connections between them. You will hopefully start to become aware of a whole rather than seeing individual concepts as being social pedagogical.

You will find examples to link theory to practice which feature a range of practitioners, carers, and so on. The application is not restricted to these areas. Examples will probably spark thoughts of relevance for your own work. One of the considerable strengths of social pedagogy is the potential it offers to a wide range of people, services, organisations and society by providing an overarching framework that connects, offering a shared language and common understandings.

We refer to people as beneficiaries of services in a variety of ways, such as service users or clients. In practice examples we use fictitious names. We may refer to adults, children and young people. We find that no one term fits all contexts as social pedagogy can work in universal services as well as services of prevention and intervention, for children, young people, families, individuals, groups, people with disabilities, adults and older people.

Some will be familiar with academic referencing, others may not. Throughout the book you will find authors' names and year of publication in brackets, which relate to the list of publications in the References section at the back of the book.

Every effort has been made to provide a rounded overview. If you have comments, suggestions or questions, please contact us. You may encounter terms or ideas that you would like to understand better, in which case please feel free to be in touch.

We are open to creating a series of pocket books relevant to the development of social pedagogy, and if you are interested in collaborating on future projects please let us know.

abby@jacaranda-development.co.uk or
manuel@jacaranda-development.co.uk

Enjoy the read!

WHAT IS SOCIAL PEDAGOGY?

Social pedagogy is an ethical, theoretical and practical approach to practice, training, education and policy. It addresses social issues in a broadly educative way (because it is more than schooling) and can work in tandem with justice and welfare approaches (Petrie et al., 2006).

Many European countries have a long history and tradition of social pedagogy. It has developed over the course of centuries and reflects in its theory and practice the work of philosophers, practitioners and key thinkers. (Sünker & Braches-Chyrek, 2009) (p.24 Key thinkers and pioneers).

1844

The term social pedagogy was coined by Karl Mager, a German educator, in 1844 (Kronen, 2001) and has since developed into an academic discipline and profession. As a university degree social pedagogy draws on theories and concepts of related subjects, such as sociology, psychology, education and philosophy.

It aims to create a more just society through educational measures and through the holistic development of individuals

---

and groups. It does so by focusing on the prevention *and* resolution of social problems (Hämäläinen, 2003).

Social pedagogy directly supports people to reach their potential, and also works towards developing an understanding of and reducing or overcoming social or structural obstacles to full participation and inclusion in community and society. It is practised in a variety of settings, ranging from early years, social care services, open youth work, and youth offending to marginalised adults, older people, people with disabilities, homeless people, and so on.

Social pedagogy is both a body of theory and a very creative and practical profession. This means making use of activities, such as music, art, arts and crafts, sport and outdoor activities. For example, a worker in a children's home may approach supporting a young person to identify and express their feelings via photography, or with a graffiti wall. The use of activities enables the practitioner and client to incorporate personal interests and strengths in the pedagogical relationship. In addition, working in a creative way encompasses creative approaches to problem solving and planning processes, as well as striving to nurture and promote creative skills in the people with whom we work. Crucially in social pedagogy there is a focus on identifying and creating opportunities for creative learning. Theory underpins the planning and development of activities. Reflection on activities will also be underpinned by theory.

The methods and specific theories of social pedagogical practice may differ according to the setting and context of the client or client group. However, practitioners will share across countries and sectors core social pedagogical principles such as humanistic values, a strengths-based approach and holding an unconditional regard for the intrinsic value of human beings (Petrie et al., 2006). Social pedagogy provides us with an ethical and value-based framework which informs and guides professional practice. (p.18 Key values and core principles; p.19 Haltung)

Social pedagogy's relationship with society is an integral part of its identity. Social pedagogy influences society and society has an impact on how social pedagogy is practised. Mollenhauer (1964) describes it as a "function of society". For example, the concept of childhood and the image of children vary from country to country and at different times in history. This is seen in services for children and the laws applicable to children, such as early years provision and the right to vote. It follows that social problems are also defined differently in different places and at different times.

Social pedagogy both reflects and critically examines the society in which it is practised in the ways it addresses social problems (Hämäläinen, 2003). This includes critically examining perceptions, values, societal norms, policies, legislation and the way society's most vulnerable members are supported. Here we touch on one of the meanings of the word "social" in social pedagogy.

Meet Christine, a support worker, who supports Emma in her transition to independence. Emma believes there should be no upper age limit and no conditions attached to support services for young people who have been in care. Christine supports Emma to attend the All Party Parliamentary Group for Looked After Children, so that Emma can express her view directly to politicians in the group. In this way, Christine enables and empowers Emma to question the existing legislation in a forum set up to hear young people's views. The MPs attending commit to exploring this further.

Historically, social pedagogical practice, theory and policy have developed in various ways according to culture and society (Hämäläinen, 2003). It is not possible to directly transfer a social pedagogical understanding from one country to another, because the way in which social pedagogy is practised will vary according to the society and culture in which it is practised. This is not to deny the core characteristics of social pedagogy which can be recognised across borders.

KEY VALUES AND CORE PRINCIPLES

Social pedagogy is underpinned by humanistic values. People are seen as active and resourceful agents, with an intrinsic potential for learning and development. Social pedagogy works holistically, seeing people as whole beings (emotional, social, moral, spiritual, physical, cognitive and so on). Service users are met with respect and a focus on strengths and potential. This is not to say that areas for development are not considered and/or acted upon.

Great emphasis is placed on *relationships* as the basis for social pedagogical work. Practitioners and service users meet not just in the context of a professional relationship, but also as human beings. Social pedagogy encourages engagement in a holistic way. For example, some aspects of the personal life of each may be intentionally used within the professional situation to build relationship. (Note, the "personal" should not be confused with the "private". (p.49 3 Ps)). A social worker may talk with a father and son about their interest in fishing when meeting them for the first time – an interest shared by the social worker, which s/he may reveal. In this way, a rapport may be established, the social worker may learn about strengths in the relationship between father and son, and so on – before moving on to the recent, concerning conflict between them.

Regular and critical (self-) reflection is a key part of the social pedagogical approach. (p.55 Reflection). This enables us to create and/or identify opportunities to learn and develop, and to adapt to changing circumstances. This is considered to be a life-long process, which involves self-challenge in order to set appropriate stimuli for personal and professional development (p.62 Learning Zone Model).

HALTUNG

"Haltung" is a German word which is finding its way into the English language, not least because there is no direct translation. It can be roughly translated as "stance", "ethos" or "inner anchor". It describes the way our actions and thinking are guided by our convictions. It can be "lived" to varying degrees. For example, you may believe in equality of opportunity and apply it in your work, and you may in addition attend demonstrations and seek to raise awareness amongst colleagues, friends and so on.

A social pedagogical "Haltung" would strive towards an empathetic understanding of people, be respectful and recognise the unconditional value of human beings. This requires a curiosity for and understanding of the reality, or life-worlds (p.42 Life-world orientation) of others. Our "Haltung" affects how we engage in relationships, having an impact on how we interact privately and professionally (Eichsteller, 2010).

"Haltung" reflects our core beliefs that are universally true and not dependent on context. It cannot be pretended; actions or words that don't reflect inner values are not authentic and might be easily detected by others. A process of self-reflection helps us to be aware of how our inner beliefs are reflected in our words and actions, and strive towards congruence between them.

EMPOWERMENT

Empowerment is core to participation and inclusion. It enables and encourages people who face obstacles to being included and participating, to increase their sense of control and be part of decisions affecting them. Empowerment aims to reduce the barriers a person faces, which may be physical, structural or institutional. It also aims to increase or develop

the sense of self-determination a person has via increased
confidence, self-belief and new or developed skills. This in
turn better equips people to address with greater autonomy
the challenges they may face in life. The methods used to
increase participation and inclusion differ depending on the
context of each person or group (Adams, 2008).

Susan is 51 years old and has been unemployed for a long
time. Her social network has reduced considerably and she
has low self-esteem. She feels defeated and spends most of the
day at home. She has a good relationship with a guidance and
career worker, Jim.

In their discussions Jim challenges Susan's convictions in order
to stimulate her commitment to change. He helps Susan to
identify her many talents and encourages her to think about
what she could do to lift her spirits. Susan is now more
motivated and wants to search the internet for contributions
she could make in the community. Jim shows her how to use
Google and how to write a letter of interest. Eventually Susan
finds a volunteering opportunity in a local day centre for the
elderly. Susan says: "This has really helped me to feel less
isolated; I have even made a few friends. I feel better about

myself and feel I am still worth something. I also realised that I have skills that I could use in work. That's a next step for me. I feel I now have more control over my life and the praise I have been given has provided me with more confidence to apply for jobs."

The following key principles of a strengths-based approach in social work, which Saleebey (2013) links to empowerment, overlap with key principles of social pedagogy:

- Every person has strengths, potential and capacity to grow and develop.

- Every environment is full of resources, which are apparent, or need uncovering.

- The practitioner or carer advocates for service users.

- Empowerment works at different levels, i.e. individual, group, organisational, community, societal and the political levels, to create a more just world.

- The practitioner or carer aims to understand and respect different life-worlds (p.42 Life-world

orientation), perceptions and coping strategies when
service users face difficulties, that may otherwise
be met with judgement as "right or wrong" (p.71
Communication; p.41 Hermeneutics).

Empowerment in practice can bring about some challenges
to people and systems. In supporting the empowerment
of another person it may be necessary to relinquish
one's own power. Also, empowering people and enabling
them to be part of decision-making processes doesn't
automatically mean that their wishes can be fulfilled. There
are limitations, such as rules, and regulations, which require
a careful explanation to ensure that responses in such
situations are not disempowering.

KEY THINKERS AND PIONEERS

We have selected a very few key thinkers, including some who pre-date the emergence of the field of social pedagogy. In this case, their work has informed social pedagogy, in the same way that contemporary thinkers could be considered to contribute the construction of a social pedagogy for the UK and Ireland. Please research further for yourself as the detail provided here is limited. Suggestions are signposted at the end of this section.

JEAN-JACQUES ROUSSEAU (1712-1778)

Rousseau was born in Switzerland but became known as a French philosopher and educationalist. At the time of his work, children were considered to be adults in the making, childhood being a necessary stage on the journey to adulthood. Children would wear adult clothing in smaller sizes and were encouraged to emulate adults' behaviour.

Rousseau thought that human beings are inherently good and closest to nature at birth, only to be corrupted by society as they grow older. He wanted to conserve the goodness in people and so based his pedagogical theory on bringing up children in accordance with nature. With his thinking and the novel "Emile" he had a significant impact on the view of childhood, and laid the foundation for the understanding of childhood as we know it today (Rousseau, 2009).

JOHANN HEINRICH PESTALOZZI (1746–1827)

Pestalozzi was also born in Switzerland and was a pedagogical philosopher who first described education as a holistic process. He moved away from filling children's heads with information and ready-made answers, and developed an approach to education that allowed children to discover answers for themselves.

His concept addressed the head, heart and hands (p.47 Head, Heart and Hands).The head represented the intellectual education, promoting a child's capacity to think. Great importance was placed on the heart, understood to be the moral education and promotion of Christian values. Without this, Pestalozzi felt the physical and intellectual capacities would not develop naturally. The hands symbolised learning via physical activities and movement as well as tactile perception. Rather than fitting prescribed moulds, children were encouraged and supported to fulfil their own ambitions (Brühlmeier, 2010).

Pestalozzi emphasised the importance of an honest and empathetic relationship between the pedagogue and the child as an essential ingredient of successful child-centred practice.

THOMAS JOHN BARNARDO (1845–1905)

Barnardo was an Irish-born philanthropist and founder of children's homes. He studied medicine, but didn't formally qualify.

In 1870, after experiencing the appalling conditions in which a lot of children lived, he founded his first children's home in London where he fed, clothed and educated poor children. His provision of a home *and* vocational training opportunities for all children, regardless of their gender, background and religious beliefs, was pioneering. He regarded religious education as key to the overall development of children and ensured they received this based on the denomination of their parents. Barnardo developed one of the first fostering schemes and boarded out babies and children of unmarried mothers, who were then also able to visit their children. (Barnardo's, no date)

MARIA MONTESSORI (1870 – 1952)

Montessori was the first woman admitted to medical school
at the University of Rome and to graduate as a doctor. She
worked with children with special needs, developing a
coherent method that was revolutionary for the time.

She later found that principles from this work could be
transferred to the general education of children. Similarly
to Rousseau, Montessori felt that children were different
to adults in how they think and develop, and had absorbent
minds and an inner drive and motivation for self-directed
learning (Lillard, 2008).

Montessori provided children with an environment that she
felt was beneficial to their learning and which, unusually
for the time, was hands-on, encouraging children to use all
their senses. One particular feature that many of us may
recall from our own childhoods was the use of small chairs
and tables in the class room, which was first introduced
by Montessori.

JANUSZ KORCZAK (1878 – 1942)

Korczak is the pen-name of Henryk Goldszmit who was born in Poland in 1878. He worked as a doctor in a Jewish hospital in Warsaw and then took a post running a Jewish orphanage. His pedagogical understanding was based on the idea that "children are not the people of tomorrow but the people of today" (Korczak, cited in Josephs, 2007, p.10). Korczak believed children have rights and should be treated with respect. This thinking was put into practice when he turned the orphanage into a children's republic. Children were involved in decision-making processes and they played an active part in staff recruitment, for example. Korczak established a children's parliament as well as a children's court. Matters that arose within the orphanage could be disputed in the court and everybody, including staff members, was bound by its decisions. This created a sense of joint and self-responsibility which took children's views into account (Lifton, 1988).

In 1940 the orphanage was forced to move into the Warsaw ghetto and in 1942 the children and Korczak were transported to the Treblinka extermination camp. Despite a number of offers to save his life, Korczak remained steadfast and accompanied the children to the last. (p.19 Haltung).

Below we have identified a few of the individuals who have pioneered social pedagogy, as an indication of the extent of its influence on thinking and development of services. Suggestions for further reading are signposted at the back of the book.

John Amos Comenius (1592 – 1670). Czech philosopher, pedagogue and theologian.

Saw the pedagogue as a gardener who nurtures the conditions for children as opposed to a sculptor who forms the child according to a pre-defined image.

Thomas Coram (1668 – 1751). Philanthropist.

Founded the London Foundling Hospital to look after abandoned children.

Robert Owen (1771 – 1858). Social reformer.

Founder of infant care in the UK. Introduced worker friendly principles in his New Lanark Mill, Scotland.

Friedrich Fröbel (1782 – 1852). Pedagogue.

Developed the concept of kindergarten.

Friedrich Adolph Wilhelm Diesterweg (1790- 1866).
Pedagogue and educational thinker.

Felt that the interests and needs of a child should be guiding principles for education so that they can develop and grow up naturally and freely.

Karl Mager (1810-1858). School pedagogue and school politician, founding father of social pedagogy.

Coined the term social pedagogy in 1844 and developed a definition for it.

Paul Natorp (1854 – 1924). Philosopher and pedagogue.

Encouraged a strong sense of community, working to close the gap between the poor and rich.

Rachel McMillan (1859 – 1917). Socialist, and **Margaret McMillan (1860 – 1931).** Socialist and politician.

Worked to improve healthcare for children, including supplying free school meals. Opened the UK's first school clinic.

Emmeline Pethick (1867 – 1954). Women's rights activist, and **Mary Neal (1860 – 1944).** Social worker.

Neal set up and ran a club for working girls, supported by Pethick.

Gertrud Bäumer (1873 – 1954). Feminist and politician.

Saw social pedagogy as everything that is education, outside the school and family.

Herman Nohl (1879 – 1960). Pedagogue and philosopher.

Believed that it was not the problems a child causes in society that should be the focus of social pedagogical intervention, but rather the problems the child experiences.

Kurt Hahn (1886 – 1974). Pedagogue and politician.

Developed the concept of
experiential education.
Involved in founding the Duke
of Edinburgh Award.

Paolo Freire (1921 – 1997). Brazilian pedagogue.

Author of "Pedagogy of the Oppressed". Criticised among
other things that education sees pupils as empty vessels
whose heads need to be filled with knowledge, rather than
promoting critical thinking and exploration.

Haydn Davies Jones (1924-2012). Early champion of
social pedagogy.

One of the first British advocates of social pedagogy.
He wrote the first book in English on the topic and also
championed high-quality residential care.

Klaus Mollenhauer (1928 – 1998). Social pedagogue.

Saw social pedagogy as a function of society which
necessarily needs to include an element of social criticism.

DEVELOPMENTS IN THE UK AND IRELAND

There are undoubtedly cultural and political reasons that during the 150 years that our European neighbours were developing the field of social pedagogy, the term remained largely unfamiliar here until recent times (Petrie, 2013). In considering pioneers from these shores such as Robert Owen and Thomas Barnardo, however, we could in hindsight apply the understanding of social pedagogy to some of their work (p.24 Key thinkers and pioneers). Montessori nurseries and schools are not unfamiliar to us and there are further examples of social pedagogical approaches, such as Pestalozzi villages. Your further reading and exploration will reveal more examples.

During the 1990s, exchange between British and European academics in the form of networks and research relating to social work, early years and school-age childcare increasingly brought our attention to social pedagogy. In the late 1990s the English Department of Health looked to social pedagogy, primarily due to concerns about outcomes for children in care. Comparative research was commissioned of the Institute of Education, and the Centre for Understanding Social Pedagogy (CUSP) was formed (Petrie, 2013).

English government interest in social pedagogy stimulated developments in practice and training. Pilots in residential care developed in-house training courses, practice exchange and modelling (Bengtsson et al., 2008; Berridge et al., 2011; Cameron et al., 2011). Jacaranda Recruitment, created in 2003 to recruit European qualified social workers and social pedagogues, recruited over 40 social pedagogues to a pilot project funded by the English Department for Children, Schools and Families, and prior to that a much smaller number to the National Centre for Excellence in Residential Child Care (NCERCC) residential pilot. During this time some university degrees started to integrate social pedagogy into their curricula, and a Masters in Social Pedagogy was created.

Since 2003, in addition to recruitment relating to the active exploration of social pedagogy, social pedagogues have been placed in a variety of work settings: children's homes, safeguarding, statutory work with looked after children, work with adults and older people, to name a few.

In 2008 ThemPra Social Pedagogy was formed, offering work-based learning and development courses and – in collaboration with colleagues at CUSP and Jacaranda – started the Social Pedagogy Development Network (SPDN).

This network provides the opportunity to meet twice yearly in rotating locations across the UK and Ireland. It is a grassroots movement that provides a forum for people who are interested in social pedagogy, and is based on social pedagogical principles such as open dialogue. Participants share experience and ideas, debate and form supportive relationships, thereby nurturing the development of social pedagogy.

Also during this time a social pedagogical perspective to a level 3 qualification was developed by Break Charity in partnership with Norfolk County Council, and Jacaranda started to offer learning and development courses in social pedagogy. Organised field trips and mobility trips enabled participants to explore social pedagogical practice and education in Germany and Denmark, facilitated by Jacaranda and ThemPra respectively.

In the early part of this decade, the Head, Heart, Hands programme, led by The Fostering Network with delivery partners the Social Pedagogy Consortium (p.40 Social Pedagogy Consortium), set about introducing social pedagogy in fostering services in England and Scotland (The Fostering Network, 2014). The programme combines the employment of social pedagogues, systemic support for change and organisational development, with ten-day courses primarily for foster carers but also some social workers and other professionals.

In 2013 the Association of Directors of Children's Services also commended social pedagogy in their position statement "What is Care For: Alternative models of care for adolescents" (ADCS, 2013).

It is noteworthy that developments in social pedagogy starting in areas such as fostering services or children's homes, have seen an extension of the development to include other service areas and professional groups. This is testimony to the broad application of social pedagogy and its potential to integrate professional groups.

In 2014 and into 2015 a number of children's homes in Ireland recruited "house pedagogues" to provide live-in care for children and young people, and elsewhere in Ireland early interest has been shown in higher education.

In Northern Ireland there has been some development of social pedagogy in a small number of organisations, and interest in higher education.

During 2015 the Care Council for Wales have explored social pedagogy in a small number of knowledge exchange seminars.

Developments more specific to Scotland include cross-sector "learning conversations" about the wider development of social pedagogy and its perceived re-ignition of a Scottish tradition in social work (Petrie, 2013). The Centre for Excellence for Looked After Children in Scotland (CELCIS) have funded courses and both the Scottish government and children's sector umbrella organisation, Children in Scotland have supported social pedagogy development.

A forum for higher education institutes to share and jointly explore further development of courses comes at the same time as the UK sees the first Chair of Social Pedagogy, Professor Claire Cameron, confirmed. Developments in higher education both mirror and complement interest in practice settings and policy arenas.

At the time of going to press, ambitions to create a four-nation Social Pedagogy Professional Association, and to develop national occupational standards and level 3 and level 5 qualifications, are being realised.

Below is a brief overview of our organisation.

JACARANDA DEVELOPMENT

Jacaranda is an ethical enterprise offering work-based learning and development courses and recruitment services in social pedagogy and social work. We support and advise organisations to develop social pedagogy and navigate implied change processes, with a focus on sustainability. We recruit social pedagogues, as well as social workers and care staff, for permanent positions. We are part of the Social Pedagogy Development Network organising group and part of the Social Pedagogy Consortium.

Below is a brief overview of just some of the organisations (and collaborations) which explore, support and nurture the overall development of social pedagogy in the UK and Ireland. There are more organisations and individuals who contribute in a variety of ways, many of whom attend the Social Pedagogy Development Network.

CENTRE FOR UNDERSTANDING SOCIAL PEDAGOGY (CUSP), UCL INSTITUTE OF EDUCATION, LONDON

Since its inception in 2009, and building on work since the late 1990s, CUSP has been a key player in inspiring and co-ordinating the impetus for social pedagogy in this country. It has done so through development work, research, teaching and regular meetings and collaboration with European academics in the field.

THEMPRA SOCIAL PEDAGOGY

ThemPra is a social enterprise supporting professionals and organisations in embedding social pedagogy. It is involved in programmes with children's residential, fostering, family and adult support services as well as EU-funded Leonardo Mobility projects. They have published book chapters and articles and co-edit the "International Journal of Social Pedagogy". They co-ordinate the Social Pedagogy Development Network and are also part of the Social Pedagogy Consortium.

BREAK CHARITY
(IN PARTNERSHIP WITH NORFOLK COUNTY COUNCIL)

Developed a social pedagogical perspective to the mandatory level 3 training qualifications for those working in children's homes and with children, young people and their families in the community.

SOCIAL PEDAGOGY CONSORTIUM (SPC)
JACARANDA, THEMPRA AND CUSP

A collective of organisations collaborating to explore, support and deliver in projects that develop social pedagogy in the UK and Ireland.

HOLISTIC PRACTICE

Holistic learning and development is a key pillar to social pedagogy and referred to throughout this book. Here we outline some particularly relevant concepts and models.

HERMENEUTICS

In a social pedagogical and a sociological context, hermeneutics is concerned with the interpretation and understanding of human actions and thinking. Different people look at the same thing differently, possibly coming to differing conclusions. In this way a person's reality is constructed, rather than being an objective fact or undisputed reality. These realities are influenced by experiences, social context and views of the world (Nohl, 1949). A person's reality can best be understood by trying to see the world through their eyes and being aware of their life-world (p.42 Life-world orientation).

The saying, "you can lead a horse to water, but you can't make it drink" reminds us that real change is unlikely to occur if it is imposed. This is also the case if a person feels misunderstood or that they are not taken seriously. Hermeneutics can help us to better understand others' thinking and behaviour, whilst engaging with them respectfully. This can have a positive effect on relationships, and on service users' commitment to make meaningful and sustainable change, which in turn is likely to have a positive impact on the social pedagogical intervention as a whole.

Hermeneutics requires active listening and observing behaviour from a non-judgemental position. We need to be aware of our own "constructions of reality" based on our life-world, and of course the impact this has on how we perceive the world around us, how our own views and values are affected and consequently how we communicate. A hermeneutical approach is supported by critical reflection to challenge our thinking, beliefs and perceptions.

LIFE-WORLD ORIENTATION

Hans Thiersch developed this concept in the late 1970s, in response to the predominantly medical approach to social pedagogy at that time. The German word "*Lebensweltorientierung*" is somewhat difficult to translate, so we have given a literal translation, aware of its unfamiliarity in the English language. It could also be translated as "life-world approach". It is based on the understanding that to support people to address and overcome their social problems, it is necessary to first understand their life-world (Grunwald & Thiersch, 2009).

Life-world includes, among other things, a person's personality, strengths, likes, dislikes, their extended family and friends, culture, religion, place of upbringing and significant events in their lives. It focuses on the person as a whole rather than only certain aspects of their lives. This holistic approach to working with a service user, for example, enables practitioners to understand the person in the context of their lives and lived experiences, rather than through the lens of their social problems. (p.41 Hermeneutics).

Also included in life-world is a person's perception of their abilities to effect change in their lives, to act independently and to make their own decisions. A service user's perception of their own ability may differ from their actual ability, or the perceptions others have. Life-world oriented practice works towards increasing a person's sense of, and their actual ability to make choices and be part of decision-making processes. This can be achieved both in direct work with a service user, for example by developing decision-making skills, or enabling an increase in confidence, and also reducing more structural obstacles that prevent participation and inclusion.

For Thiersch, respect for the individual's life plans and ways of approaching difficulties and coping with adversity was of great importance. Practitioners were encouraged to strive to understand and respect this even when the direction may go against generally held perceptions of "right and wrong". This can be challenging for practitioners whose role includes advocating on behalf of the service user. A lived understanding of life-world can have a positive effect on the relationship between practitioner and service user, as well as promoting an increased sense of control and self-determination, which can promote positive outcomes and change.

Understanding a service user's life-world can enable a practitioner in the important dimension of social pedagogy which goes beyond direct work with people, namely seeking to proactively influence structures and systems that play a role in the social problems they face. In this way, people are supported both as individuals and on a structural level. (p.20 Empowerment; p.13 What is social pedagogy).

DIAMOND MODEL

This model (Eichsteller & Holthoff, 2012) describes one of the core principles of social pedagogy: the unconditional value of human beings. Social pedagogy recognises that everyone has an intrinsic worth and possesses a unique set of skills, abilities and talents, which may not at first be seen – similar to a diamond in the rough. Social pedagogy recognises the potential for further growth and supports people to develop further and to work towards reaching their full potential. There are four core aims that are closely interlinked:

Well-being and happiness

Eichsteller and Holthoff (2012) see it as the overarching aim of social pedagogy to provide people with well-being and happiness. Happiness can be seen as something momentary and linked to the present whereas well-being is a more longer-lasting state that incorporates physical, mental, emotional and social factors. As perceptions of both are highly subjective, social pedagogical practice needs to be context-specific.

Holistic learning

Academic education is only one part of learning. Learning is considered a life-long process that involves the person as a whole (p.47 Head, Heart and Hands) and contributes to a

person's well-being. Social pedagogy consciously seeks to
create and identify situations in which learning can occur,
often making use of everyday situations.

Relationships

Strong relationships are the foundation of social pedagogical
practice and directly contribute to achieving the previous two
aims. In order to support a person we need to understand
their life-world (p.42 Life-world orientation) and the
challenges they may face. Social pedagogy encourages us
to use our personal self, alongside our professional capacity
(p.49 3 Ps) to form authentic relationships.

Empowerment

Empowerment describes the process of enabling people
to take greater ownership and control of their lives, for
example via awareness of their rights and/or an increase
in their confidence. Social pedagogy supports people to
play an active part in decisions that affect them and to feel
more responsible for their own development, well-being and
happiness and relationship with the community.

Positive experiences

Providing positive experiences is essential to strengthening and developing these four core aims. Positive experiences – such as knowing that someone supports you or something you have learned or achieved – can have a direct impact on increasing self-esteem, feeling empowered and achieving a more positive self-image. This in turn strengthens our sense of well-being and happiness.

HEAD, HEART AND HANDS

Pestalozzi's Head, Heart and Hands advocates that we learn and act using our head (cognitive, knowledge), heart (emotions, morals) and hands (behaviour or actions) (Brühlmeier, 2010). We may notice a natural leaning to one or the other in ourselves and others, and this may vary according to predisposition and context, such as if we are at work or at home or how energised we feel. People who are governed by their **head** tend to lean towards thought, and draw on their experiences and theoretical knowledge. People who are more governed by their **heart** tend to follow their intuition and impulses and to consider feelings more. If you are driven by your **hands** you might enjoy practical activities – the doing and acting. We all have all three elements, but we may also have a natural predisposition towards one or the other. In addition to this, professional roles often come with an expectation of emphasis in one area, more than others. For example, a manager may have started their career in a children's home and enjoy practical work (emphasis on hands, but not excluding head and heart). The responsibilities linked to their management role could be perceived as having a leaning towards the head, but may be enhanced by considering all three areas.

Social pedagogy strives for a balance between the head, heart and hands by promoting the development of all three areas. This concept can be seen as a dynamic reflection and practice tool, to identify and apply areas of strength as well as promoting development. By reflecting on the Head, Heart and Hands model, a person may respond according to the situation, where an emphasis in one area may be more appropriate over another.

Meet James, a children's social worker, who is on a home visit to speak to the parents of one of the children he is working with. Mum, Jane, tells him that she is at the end of her tether as her son is verbally abusive towards her and has twice threatened to stab her. James is governed by his head;

> he tends to try to find explanations, linking to theory and his
> professional experience. James has learned about the Head,
> Heart and Hands model in social pedagogy training. This has
> made him aware of predispositions and how this may affect
> his practice. He feels that over-theorising would not be helpful
> in this situation and decides to listen to Jane empathetically
> (heart) as well as focusing on suitable actions to address this
> behaviour (hands), whilst still using his theoretical knowledge.
> After the home visit, he reflects on the conversation using the
> Head, Heart and Hands model to analyse his response.

3 PS

The 3 Ps is a Danish concept that introduces the idea that we
could all be seen to consist of three spheres: the professional,
the personal and the private (Jappe, 2010).

The **professional** draws on, for example, knowledge,
theory, research, evidence and experience to assess and
respond to situations. It enables us to work with people in a
professional framework, to achieve goals and objectives.

The **personal** should be seen as distinct from the private.
Sharing something of ourselves, in a reflective way, means

the person with whom we are working sees that we too
are human, having our own preferences, experiences,
challenges and so on. This helps to build authentic
relationships, which is important as social pedagogy is a
relational approach. The relationship forms the foundation
of work and a basis for its success. Appropriately sharing
something personal may help to reduce imbalances
of power and help us to connect on a
human level. If a service user has a
dog, for example, you might share your
own experience of raising a dog, funny
moments and so on. Deciding what can be
shared with whom requires careful reflection.

The **private** refers to that area of life which we would share
only with those close to us, if at all. Inappropriately sharing
such information may put us in a vulnerable position, and
careful consideration of the difference between the personal
and the private is very important. Where the line is drawn
between the two depends on the kind of information, the
context and whether something positive might come from
sharing in a professional relationship. Social pedagogy
encourages a reflective and conscious use of all three
spheres to create a safe space for everyone, which is full of
learning opportunities.

Kate fosters Brian, a teenager. They regularly get into heated discussions regarding Brian's alcohol consumption. Kate is very strict and has a "no tolerance policy". Kate lost a family member due to alcohol abuse. Ordinarily Kate and her supervising social worker may feel that this fact belongs in the private sphere. There may, however, be value in sharing something of this story with Brian to help him better understand her strong views around alcohol. This may help them reach a compromise and may improve the relationship.

Meet Sheila, who provides supported lodgings, and David, the young person she is supporting. Sheila's best friend and neighbour has recently lost a close family member and is grieving. David is apprehensive about independence, and at the moment memories of his feelings when he was removed from his birth parents are very real. Sharing the reason why Sheila is spending more time with her close friend and her sense of loss and sadness with David *could* have a negative effect on him. In this case it might make more sense to keep this in the private sphere.

Kate and Sheila regularly use the 3 Ps as a reflective tool to assess where boundaries are and whether sharing certain things could benefit the relationships or support the young people they care for.

COMMON THIRD

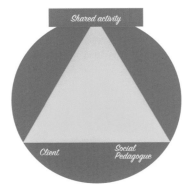

The Common Third (Lihme, 1988) is a very practical concept that enables us to strengthen relationships, learn from each other and develop new skills. It also highlights the importance in working relationships of the conscious use of activities and environments, such as a walk in the park or driving in a car. Such activities need not be elaborate or resource-intensive. Cooking, or driving locally, could be just as effective as a trip to France!

When two people undertake an activity together, or find themselves in a different environment, the focus is on the task or place rather than directly on each other, creating a more relaxed atmosphere. (Lihme, 1988). The interaction is not specifically about the past, or plans for the future, but about swimming, cycling or cooking, for example. The relationship may be enhanced during the activity and more may emerge that supports, for example, an intervention or a dialogue supporting a placement, than might otherwise be the case.

Self-challenge and life-long learning are both important in the Common Third. An activity might be chosen that particularly interests a young person, for example, about which the practitioner or carer may know very little, or nothing at all. This may reverse the "usual" power dynamics. The young person can take responsibility in showing and possibly encouraging the adult, which could positively impact on the young person's confidence and self-esteem.

Activities may be fun, but crucially there is intention and method which characterises the Common Third, i.e. there is a conscious use of method, which includes planning, carrying out and reflecting on an activity.

Dai, a young person with disabilities, lives in a children's home. He has low self-esteem and confidence. His key worker, Morven, wants to support him and thinks about a suitable Common Third activity. Morven is not confident in using Facebook and Whatsapp and wonders if Dai may grow in confidence by teaching her something about social media.

Dai agrees and they start with a few sessions. Dai is more knowledgeable than Morven and so the "traditional" roles within their relationship are reversed. Dai is taking a different kind of responsibility in this activity. Morven later reflects with Dai on how well he has been teaching her and within a debrief they talk about how he may transfer his increased self-esteem into other areas, such as college work or social interactions.

REFLECTION

Many of the concepts we outline in this pocket book can be used in reflective processes, such as the understandings of how we communicate, Head, Heart and Hands and hermeneutics. The Learning Zone Model and an unconditional positive regard help us to approach reflection with openness to learning and respect for the strengths and potential of others and ourselves. This can help us to raise our awareness of any feelings of defensiveness we may have, and help us consider how we respond in the light of them. Reflection is an important element of personal, professional and practice development.

CRITICAL REFLECTION

Critical reflection enables us to analyse and evaluate our practice with some depth. Often we hear that reflection takes place whilst driving home, or thinking whilst doing something else. Critical reflection is a more structured and deeper process, more than thinking alone. It examines communication, our own assumptions, what methods have been used and why, what unintended consequences may result from a given intervention, what power is held by whom, and how it is used. It also looks at the wider organisational or societal context and considers what influences are at work. You will find suggestions for further reading signposted at the end of the book.

Critical reflection does require time, and it may also require courage if it is new to us. It plays a central role in the development of practice, and in a quality assurance for practice. Providing for the structural use of time for critical reflection, and crucially the incorporation into practice of what is learned in the process, is a key feature of a learning organisation.

Critical reflection in teams or groups brings the benefits of multiple perspectives. It can also be done individually or in smaller groups, perhaps using the written word or creative methods, or with a supervisor, mentor or peer.

Here are two models. There are more you may know of, or discover in your further reading. The 4Fs model supports reflective practice. The peer group case reflection supports a deeper process of critical reflection.

4 Fs (Greenaway, 1992):

Greenaway's 4Fs is a model which can aid learning from experience. It enables people to review and analyse a situation, meeting or event for example. People can acknowledge and describe their feelings, consider what they may learn and then focus on future actions or changes in approach or method. This model can be used individually or in groups. It can also be effectively applied in work with clients such as young people, as a practical way of reviewing and reflecting.

The 4Fs are: facts, feelings, findings and futures.

Facts: an objective description of what has happened, keeping to the facts only.

Feelings: a description of the feelings connected to the facts.

Findings: what sense can we make of the facts and the feelings? What do we learn having looked at the facts and feelings?

Futures: what can we do better or differently next time?

Peer group case reflection (6-10 people)
(Kopp & Vonesch, 2003)

This is a reflection and consultation tool that can help to
identify solutions to professional questions or dilemmas.
It draws on the expertise and experience of peers and is
characterised by a sequence of defined stages. It could be
beneficial, for example, for social workers, foster carers and
people working in children's homes. It could also be used by
a group of young people who would like to address an issue
without staff assistance, for instance.

- One person presents a problem/case, and one
  moderator keeps time, ensuring focus.

- The case is presented, together with one specific
  question e.g. how can we support this placement?

- The group asks clarifying questions to better understand
  the case.

- Ideas are exchanged within the group. The presenter of
  the case listens and is not involved in the discussion.

- Double-check: did we miss anything?

■ The presenter of the case describes what s/he found useful, what s/he would like to implement and how s/he would like to approach the situation.

JOHARI WINDOW

The Johari window is a reflection tool which promotes inter-personal understanding, self or team development. It was developed in 1955 by Joseph Luft and Harry Ingham (Johari being a combination of both names).

In the model, there are four areas that could be seen as the windowpanes:

Arena	Blind spot
(open)	(blind)
Façade	The unknown
(hidden)	(unknown)

Let's explore the model using the example of Steven, a young man arriving at a children's home for the first time.

1. Arena: There will be things the staff and others
    know about Steven, things that he too knows. Simple
    examples are his name and hair colour. The "arena"
    could also include parts of his life story, some key
    people in his life, and some likes and dislikes.

2. Blind spot: We may know something about Steven that
    he himself doesn't. It could be a note stuck to his back,
    or the fact that his neck goes red when a particular
    carer talks to him.

3. Façade: Steven may keep things from us, he knows
    things about himself that he doesn't want others to
    know. This could be insecurities, or even abuse that he
    suffered in the past.

4. Unknown: this area captures things that may be
    unknown to Steven and also unknown to others. This
    might include where he will live in the future, or whether
    he will study, or marry, but also things that happened
    in his past of which he and others may not be aware.
    This area can relate to both past and future; the latter
    containing hope as well as potential for his development.

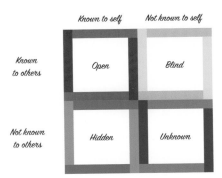

This model can be used to increase the "arena" by providing feedback and thereby reducing the "blind spot"; by sharing information or perspectives and thereby reducing the "façade" and planning and exploring the future together, so reducing the "unknown".

The Johari window is helpful in becoming more self-aware and increasing our understanding of others. Careful consideration and critical reflection are needed in deciding how to use the model, particularly in reducing blind spots where there may be sensibilities, or even revelations which may need some digesting.

APPROACHES TO LEARNING

It is important in social pedagogy to identify and create situations in which it is impossible *not* to learn (author unknown, cited in Eichsteller & Holthoff, 2012). We need to understand what supports and what hinders successful learning processes, where learning is understood in a wider sense than schooling and applies equally to services users as it does to carers, practitioners, managers and so on. The following models not only elaborate approaches to learning in practice, but can also be considered as reflective tools.

LEARNING ZONE MODEL

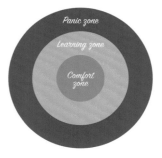

The model consists of three spheres: the comfort zone, the learning zone and the panic zone (Senninger, 2000).

The **comfort zone** is where we feel at ease with what we are doing and where we are. We know what to do, how to do it and are able to deal with anything that may arise. It is a very comfortable place, but may not be very stimulating.

In order to learn we need to leave the comfort zone and venture into more unfamiliar terrain: the **learning zone**. Here we may feel challenged, which enables us to grow and develop, to explore and learn. It is not as easy as the comfort zone, but we don't feel overwhelmed.

Beyond the learning zone lies the **panic zone**. If we venture into this zone we find ourselves unable to learn because we feel threatened, anxious or scared. We may even experience damaging learning.

Encouraging ourselves or others to explore the learning zone is beneficial. We need to avoid entering the panic zone to avoid any negative impact on our learning or confidence. We should also consider that the learning zone for one person may be for the next person a panic zone. Someone very scared of heights will regard a climbing wall in a different way to someone who has never climbed before, but is not scared of heights. Our unconditional regard for people and application of hermeneutics (p.41 Hermeneutics) are helpful here.

Lynn is a supervising social worker and mentions in supervision the challenging behaviour of one of the children, Bahia, recently placed with Fatima, a foster carer she supervises. Lynn and her manager consider this using the Learning Zone Model. Lynn reflects that Bahia, who has had some very traumatic experiences, may not be accustomed to the quiet and cleanliness of the foster home. She may feel very uncomfortable and unsure about how to be in this environment. For Bahia, a more chaotic environment is more comfortable and she recreates this in how she behaves with Fatima. Lynn sees that what may seem safe, protective and comfortable to her, may leave some people feeling uncomfortable, and may even feel threatening. She shares this in supervision with Fatima who finds this helpful in understanding Bahia's behaviour.

KOLB'S LEARNING CYCLE

Kolb's experiential learning theory (1984) is based on the understanding that we learn through experience. However learning does not automatically occur every time one has an experience; it is important to reflect to identify key points and concepts that can then be applied to new situations.

Kolb's learning cycle is based on his experiential learning theory and comprises a number of elements. Here we outline only the four stages. According to Kolb a learner would ideally go through all four stages in order for learning to be effective. It is also possible to enter the learning cycle at any stage, as long as progression through the cycle follows the suggested logical order.

Concrete experience (feeling):

This is a new practical action or something people have experienced before.

Reflective Observation (watching):

People reflect on the experience and assess it rationally.

Abstract conceptualisation (thinking):

Here people try to analyse what has happened, linking the experience and the observation to previous experiences, theories or knowledge in general.

Active experimentation (doing):

A plan is devised of how to act in a similar situation based on the learning from the previous three stages. This is then put into practice and the learning cycle starts from the beginning.

This tool is particularly useful for individual learning processes which are based on concrete experiences. It can also be put into practice by professionals working with children or adults to create more suitable learning and reflective experiences.

You will find how Kolb further developed this model, including four associated learning styles, in the further reading suggested at the end of this book.

ZONE OF PROXIMAL DEVELOPMENT (ZPD)

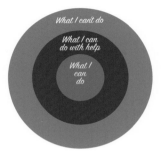

Learning doesn't take place in a vacuum. Humans are social beings and learn in a social context, in interaction with others (Vygotsky, 1978).

Lev Vygotsky, whose main work was in developmental psychology, considered social interaction very effective in developing skills and abilities. In work with children, he distinguished three areas:

■   What a child can do without support

■   What a child can do with support

■   What a child cannot do

Vygotsky described the ZPD as the area between children's individual performance and their assisted performance. Children can achieve more with assistance than they can on their own. With the support from a more advanced member of the peer group or a teacher, the so-called "more knowledgeable other", they are able to achieve more and so increase their abilities and skills. Children develop and can master a task independently, increasing the areas in which no support is needed. For Vygotsky the best way to promote children's learning and development was to engage them in their ZPD rather than aiming directly at their ability to approach a task independently.

Although Vygotsky never did so, the term "scaffolding" is often used with the ZPD. Once a child masters new skills and abilities, the scaffolding is no longer necessary and can be removed (Wood & Ross, 1976).

Working in the ZPD has implications for practice as the emphasis is more on interactional support and learning. The "more knowledgeable other" becomes more of a companion and equal, which generates a more relaxed and effective learning environment. Use of the model requires a good understanding of existing skills and areas to develop to plan and choose appropriate support. Although Vygotsky focused on children in his work, the ZPD is also relevant for learning processes for adults, such as the support provided to a newly approved foster carer by a peer.

RESILIENCE

When we adapt, cope with and overcome adversity, we are said to be resilient. Adversity could be traumatic childhood experiences such as abuse or rejection, or life stressors such as the loss of a job. Some people seem to be more resilient than others, but resilience can be learnt and further developed (Gilligan, 2009). It is for this reason that we include resilience in this section on learning.

Internal factors such as self-confidence, and external factors such as a supportive relationship, can have an impact on a person's resilience. These are known as protective factors (Masten et al., 1990). These include:

■   A positive self-image and sense of self-worth

■   Problem-solving skills

■   Feeling able to seek help

- Being supported by community

- Identifying positives in challenging experiences

- A strong relationship with family, friends and/or other significant adults

We can work consciously and with intent to strengthen these characteristics and experiences, considering what is appropriate in the context and for each individual.

COMMUNICATION

Effective communication lies at the heart of social pedagogy; it enables us to understand perspectives and to build relationships. Here we introduce some communication theories but in your further exploration you will discover more.

WATZLAWICK'S COMMUNICATION AXIOMS

An axiom is a statement which is regarded as being established, accepted or self-evidently true, though difficult to prove.

Paul Watzlawick and peers studied how people communicate and identified five axioms that underpin human communication and provide the basis for human interaction (Watzlawick et al., 1967). We interpret this as follows:

1. Axiom: you cannot **not** communicate. No matter what we do, whether we speak or not, we are always communicating. Messages can be conveyed and interpreted by words and by non-verbal communication such as gestures, eye contact, or lack of it. Sometimes the lack of words communicates messages, which may or may not reflect what we are intending to communicate.

2. Axiom: Every communication has a content and
    relationship aspect. The relationship between people
    shapes how the content of a message is spoken and
    how it is understood. The same content, "It is late."
    for example, is likely to be said and heard differently
    according to the relationship between the speaker
    and the hearer. Friends, or strangers, may hear, "It
    is late." as a statement of fact, relating more to the
    content. Between partners, "It is late." may be heard as
    containing another message, such as "It is late and I'm
    annoyed (or tired)."

3. Axiom: The punctuation in communication defines the
    relationship. According to Watzlawick, communication
    is in circular motion, having no real starting point.
    Sometimes, however conversations become "cyclic". Is
    this a familiar pattern?

    Ann: "Have you remembered to ...?"

    Ben: "Oh, I'd forgotten. Yes, yes, don't nag, I'll do it".

    Ann: "You never remember ..."

Ben: "You are always "*reminding*" me, I don't need
to remember."

Ann: "I only remind you because you always forget"

And so on...

When in cyclic communication, each person may believe
the other to be responsible for a starting point, seeing
themselves as being merely responsive. In this way
responsibility for misunderstandings may be laid at the
door of the other.

How the speaker and the listener view each other, and
their relationship, can become defined by this kind
of communication. It takes only one to put a different
"punctuation" to the communication. For example, Ann
could say "I'm sure you've remembered..." and Ben
could say, "Thank you, where would I be without you?"

4. Axiom: communication is both verbal and non-verbal.
    Communication is congruent when both the verbal and
    non-verbal communication match. "I'm so pleased
    for you." with a smile towards the face of the other
    person, making eye contact and the tone of voice

all communicating a genuine feeling, is congruent. Communication is more complex, problematic even, when verbal messages don't match non-verbal communication such as facial gestures or eye contact.

5.   Axiom: communication can be symmetrical or complementary. In our communication, we can convey how we see another person and our "power" in relation to them, in a variety of ways, including tone, body language and so on. The power may be seen as equal, or one having lesser power and the other more.

Symmetrical communication is when communication power is the same in each party. This could be the basis of equality and a feature of a healthy relationship, or it could be when each party tries to dominate, which is an ineffective communication.

Complementary communication is when the communication styles are different; for example one is more powerful than the other. This may be a situation in which one person dominates and another is submissive, which is not a healthy pattern. It could also be a result of a process of empowerment, such as if a young person in care has been empowered to speak up for themselves in a review meeting and the social worker takes a back seat, enabling them to do so.

NONVIOLENT COMMUNICATION

The concept of nonviolent communication was developed by Marshall Rosenberg in the 1960s to enable people to communicate more effectively and reduce conflicts in a peaceful way (Rosenberg, 2003). The focus is to build a relationship that is based on compassion and cooperation as well as promoting dialogue between people. Listening empathetically and expressing oneself honestly are key components.

There are four key steps:

Observation:

A description of the facts one has observed without injecting any moral judgement or evaluation.

Feelings:

We state what the above described behaviour has made us feel. It may take practice to recognise one's own feelings and to describe them accurately.

Needs:

Those feelings are connected to needs that we would like to see fulfilled. It is important to acknowledge and recognise those needs.

Request:

The aim of this step is to express the needs and say what specific action we would like to see. We accept that the needs may not be met in so doing.

Non-violent communication is more than just a way of communicating; it is a lens through which we understand and relate to other human beings more compassionately. This language of life (Rosenberg, 2003) enables us to connect more deeply to others through being empathetic and having more self-empathy which can lead to a greater authenticity in our communication.

4-SIDES MODEL

The 4-sides model, which is partly based on Watzlawick's work, was developed by Friedemann Schulz von Thun (1981). It provides a tool to analyse and improve our communication.

Let's analyse the following message using the model:

"The floor is dirty."

According to the model, there are 4 dimensions to any message: a factual element, an appeal, a relationship element and something about the speaker, said to be self-revelation.

1. **Factual**: This states the facts, in this case: the floor is dirty.

2. **Appeal/request**: This is a request within the message, here it might be: "Please clean the floor."

3. **Relationship**: The message will be understood differently depending on the relationship between people and how they relate. This message could be a form of nagging, or it could also be an observation. The context, tone of voice and so on would tell us more.

4. **Self-revelation**: Every message reveals something about the person who says it. In this case, it might show for example how observant they are, or their standards of cleanliness.

According to Schulz von Thun, every message can be spoken and heard in these 4 different ways. Misunderstandings or even hurt feelings may arise if, for example, the speaker is making a factual observation but the listener hears a request. Ideally all parties to a communication should check messages and ensure they are understood in the way they were intended.

Residential child care worker Gloria says to teenage resident Devante, "Devante, we are leaving in 10 minutes!" Ten minutes later Devante is still playing on the Xbox and Gloria is impatient. Devante, understood her message factually i.e. we are leaving in 10 minutes. What Gloria more likely meant was, "Switch off the Xbox, brush your teeth, put on some shoes, grab your coat and make sure you are ready to leave in 10 minutes."

In this case, Gloria could have adapted her communication to Devante by asking him to take all the necessary steps to get ready to leave, instead of expecting him to interpret her message. Either Devante or Gloria could also have double-checked whether the message had been understood as it was intended.

WHERE NEXT?

This pocket book on social pedagogy is written to provide a diverse readership with an introduction to the approach, its practical application and an invitation to learn more.

There is so much more to learn than we have been able – or indeed would want to attempt – to cover here. Reading is one way to learn, and the multi-dimensional nature of experience, exploring in dialogue with knowledgeable others (p.67 Zone of Proximal Development), experiential learning, creative activities and courses are other ways we advocate highly.

In the learning and development groups of our courses, theories and concepts are applied to practice, and participants also learn from each other. Often new supportive networks form. We find that ways of thinking, ways of viewing things, and consequently ways of doing things, change.

It is in these groups that we can look at how other models and approaches relate to social pedagogy. There are strong synergies and overlaps with other strengths-based and systemic approaches, and many favoured models fit well within a social pedagogy framework.

You will have gleaned that social pedagogy is not confined to direct practice; our practice sits in wider organisational contexts, which in turn sit in still wider societal, political and cultural contexts. Our work goes beyond learning and development courses in that we look at systems and change processes, recognising that whilst there is resonance which builds on current practice, there are also at times points of difference – which implies change. In partnership, we can explore what implications and opportunities there are for practice and local policies. Understandings of systems theories, of culture and of change management are integral to our approach to social pedagogy development. This means we are working in partnership and considering the organisational conditions which are supportive to the development of social pedagogy, before, during and beyond our work together.

You will find suggestions for further reading and other ways to learn more about social pedagogy in the next section. If you would like to further explore with us any aspects of what you have read, please feel free to be in touch.

abby@jacaranda-recruitment.co.uk, 020 3384 0989
manuel@jacaranda-recruitment.co.uk

FURTHER READING AND EXPLORATION

Please go to **jacaranda-development.co.uk** and see:

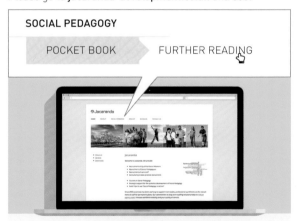

This section is online to enable us to continuously update the list as more and more resources become available in a fast-developing area.

REFERENCES

Adams, R., 2008. Empowerment, participation and social work. Basingstoke: Palgrave Macmillan.

Association of Directors of Children's Services, 2013. ADCS position statement what is care for: Alternative models of care for adolescents. [pdf] Manchester: ADCS. Available at: http://www.adcs.org.uk/download/position-statements/2013/ADCS_position_statement_What_Is_Care_For_April_2013.pdf [Accessed 14 May 2015].

Barnardo's, no date. The history of Barnardo's. [online] Available at: http://www.barnardos.org.uk/barnardo_s_history.pdf [Accessed 27 April 2015].

Bengtsson, E., Chamberlain, C., Crimmens, D. and Stanley, J., 2008. Introducing social pedagogy into residential child care in England: An evaluation of a project commissioned by the Social Education Trust. [pdf] London: Social Education Trust and National Centre for Excellence in Residential Child Care. Available at: http://www.ncb.org.uk/media/520971/introducing_sp_into_rcc_in_england_feb08.pdf [Accessed 7 May 2015].

Berridge, D., Biehal, N., Lutman, E., Henry, L. and Palomares, M., 2011. Raising the bar? Evaluation of the social pedagogy pilot programme in residential children's homes. London: Department for Education.

Brühlmeier, A., 2010. Head, heart and hand: Education in the spirit of Pestalozzi. Cambridge, UK: Open Book Publishers.

Cameron, C., Petrie, P., Wigfall, V., Kleipoedszus, S. and Jasper, A., 2011. Final report of the social pedagogy pilot programme: development and implementation. [pdf] London: Thomas Coram Research Unit, Institute of Education, University of London. Available at: http://eprints.ioe.ac.uk/6767/1/Cameron2011Final%28Report%29. pdf [Accessed 7 May 2015].

Eichsteller, G., 2010. The notion of 'Haltung' in social pedagogy. [online] Available at: http://www.childrenwebmag.com/articles/social-pedagogy/the-notion-of-%E2%80%98haltung-in-social-pedagogy [Accessed 20 April 2015].

Eichsteller, G. and Holthoff, S., 2012. The art of being a social pedagogue: Developing cultural change in children's homes in Essex. International journal of social pedagogy, 1(1), pp.30-46. [online] Available at: http://umaine.edu/socialwork/files/2014/10/ TheArtofBeingaSocialPedagoge.pdf [Accessed 12 May 2015].

Gilligan, R., 2009. Promoting resilience: A resource guide on working with children in the care system. London: British Association for Adoption and Fostering.

Greenaway, R., 1992. Reviewing by doing. Journal of adventure education and outdoor leadership. [online] Available at: http://reviewing.co.uk/articles/2rbd.htm [Accessed 20 April 2015].

Grunwald, K. and Thiersch, H., 2009. The concept of the 'lifeworld orientation' for social work social care. Journal of social work practice, 23, pp.131-146.

Hämäläinen, J., 2003. The concept of social pedagogy in the field of social work. Journal of social work, 3(1), pp.69-80.

Jappe, E., 2010. Håndbog for paedagogstuderende. Frederiksberg C: Frydenlund.

Josephs, S. ed., 2007. Loving every child: Wisdom for parents – the words of Janusz Korczak. New York: Thorsons.

Kolb, D., 1984. Experiential learning: Experience as the source of learning and development. Englewood Cliffs, NJ: Prentice-Hall.

Kopp, R. and Vonesch, L., 2003. Die Methodik der Kollegialen Fallberatung. In: Franz, H.W. and Kopp, R., eds. Kollegiale Fallberatung – state of the art und organisationale Praxis. 2nd ed. Köln: Ehp. pp.53-93.

Kronen, H., 2001. Sozialpädagogik. Geschichte und Bedeutung des Begriffs. Hanau: Haag & Herchen.

Lifton, B. J., 1988. The king of children: A biography of Janusz Korczak. London: Chatto & Windus.

Lihme, B., 1988. *Socialpædagogikken for børn og unge: et debatoplæg med særligt henblik på døgninstitutionen*. Holte: Socpol.

Lillard, R. S., 2008. Montessori: The science behind the genius. Oxford: University Press.

Luft, J. and Ingham, H., 1955. The Johari window, a graphic model of interpersonal awareness. Proceedings of the western training laboratory in group development. Los Angeles: UCLA.

Masten, A. S., Best, K. M. and Garmezy, N., 1990. Resilience and development: Contributions from the study of children who overcome adversity. Development and Psychopathology. 2 (4), pp.425–444.

Mollenhauer, K. (1964). Einführung in die Sozialpädagogik. Weinheim: Beltz Verlag.

Nohl, H., 1949. Charakter und Schicksal. Frankfurt: Verlag Gerhard Schulte Bulmke.

Petrie, P., 2013. Social pedagogy in the UK: Gaining a firm foothold? Education policy analysis archives, 21(37), [online] Available at: http://epaa.asu.edu/ojs/article/view/1339/1104 [Accessed 5 May 2015].

Petrie, P., Boddy, J., Cameron, C., Wigfall, V. and Simon, A., 2006. Working with Children in Care – European Perspectives. Maidenhead: Open University Press.

Rosenberg, M. B., 2003. Nonviolent communication: a language of life. Encinitas: Puddle Dancer Press.

Rousseau, J.J., 2009. Emile, or on education. Las Vegas: IAP.

Saleebey, D., 2013. Introduction: Power in the people. In: Saleebey, D., ed. *The strength perspective in social work practice*. 6th ed. Upper Saddle River: Pearson Education. pp. 1-24.

Senninger, T., 2000. Abenteuer leiten – in Abenteuern lernen: Methodenset zur Planung und Leitung kooperativer Lerngemeinschaften für Training und Teamentwicklung in Schule, Jugendarbeit und Betrieb. Münster: Ökotopia Verlag.

Schulz von Thun, F., 1981. Miteinander reden 1: Störungen und Klärungen. Reinbek: Rowohlt Taschenbuch Verlag.

Sünker, H. and Braches-Chyrek, R., 2009. Social pedagogy in Germany. In: Kornbeck, J. & Rosendal Jensen, N., eds. Studies in comparative social pedagogies and international social work and social policy, Vol. VII: The diversity of social pedagogy in Europe. Bremen: Europäischer Hochschulverlag, pp.12-34.

The Fostering Network, 2014. Head, Heart, Hands – Positive signs at the halfway point. [pdf] London: The Fostering network. Available at: https://www.fostering.net/sites/www.fostering.net/files/head-heart-hands-positive-signs-at-the-halfway-point.pdf [Accessed 26 April 2015].

Vygotsky, L. S., 1978. Mind in society: development of higher psychological processes. Cambridge, MA: Harvard University Press.

Watzlawick, P., Beavin Bavelas, J. and Jackson, D.D., 1967. Pragmatics of human communication: a study of interactional patterns, pathologies, and paradoxes. New York: Norton.

Wood, D., Bruner, J.S and Ross, G., 1976. The role of tutoring in problem solving. Journal of child psychology and child psychiatry, 17, pp.89–100.

ABOUT THE CONTRIBUTORS

Author's critical friend

Rob Braun is a social pedagogue and social worker, facilitator and consultant with Jacaranda Development. He graduated from the University of Applied Sciences in Aachen, in 2005. He holds a BA in Social Work from South University Maastricht and an MA in Comparative European Social Studies from London Metropolitan University. His practice experience in Germany and the Netherlands includes a variety of youth work settings and he has extensive experience in children's social work in the UK, as a practitioner and manager.

Editor

Abby Ladbrooke founded Jacaranda with Ingolf Block in 2003. She graduated in German Studies from Manchester University in 1995. Abby worked in intercultural exchange and language-travel in a variety of roles. At the time of founding Jacaranda, Abby explored social pedagogy, feeling it to be an excellent fit with the then policy agenda and finding a strong resonance with her own *Haltung*.

Editor's critical friend

Doug Lawson qualified as a social worker in 1975 and spent many years employed as a practitioner and manager in children's social care services in English local authorities. He has a particular interest in services for children in care. Since 2009 he has been working as an independent consultant, trainer and researcher.